I Can Stay Calm

Dealing with Stress

Ava Beasley

I0808940

SOCIAL AND EMOTIONAL LEARNING FOR THE REAL WORLD™

Rosen Classroom™

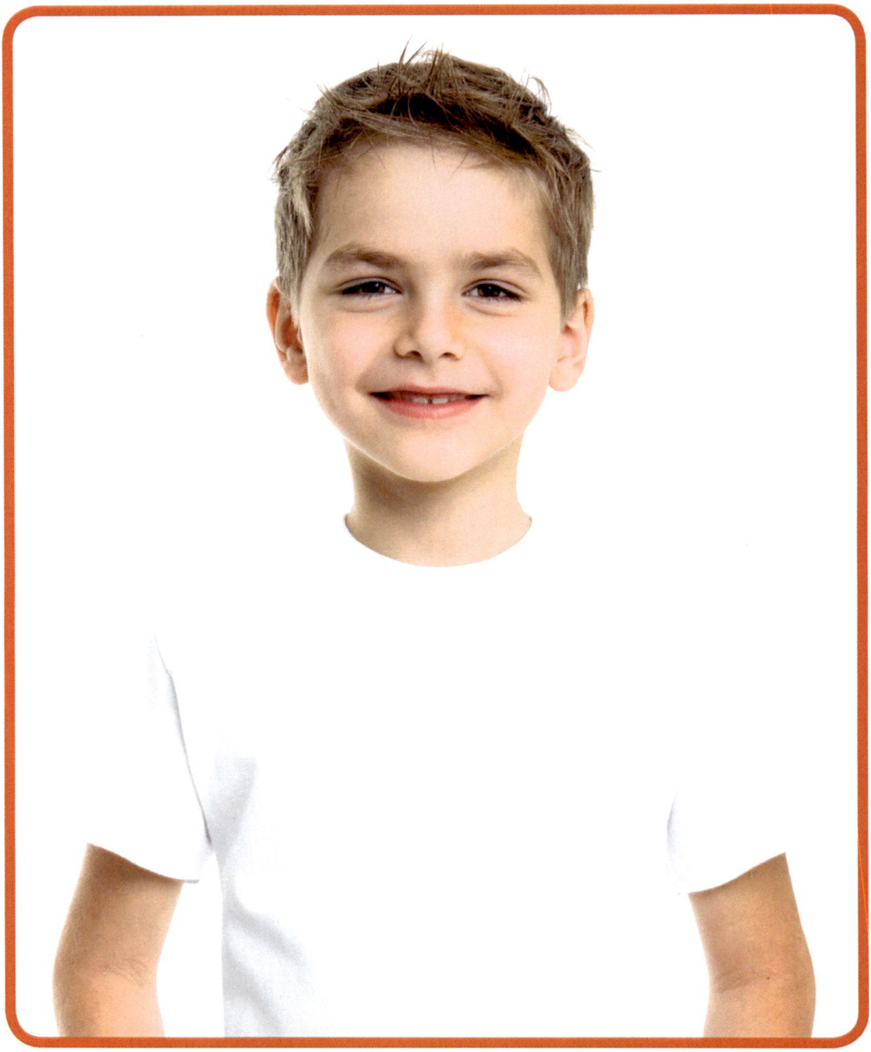

I can stay calm.

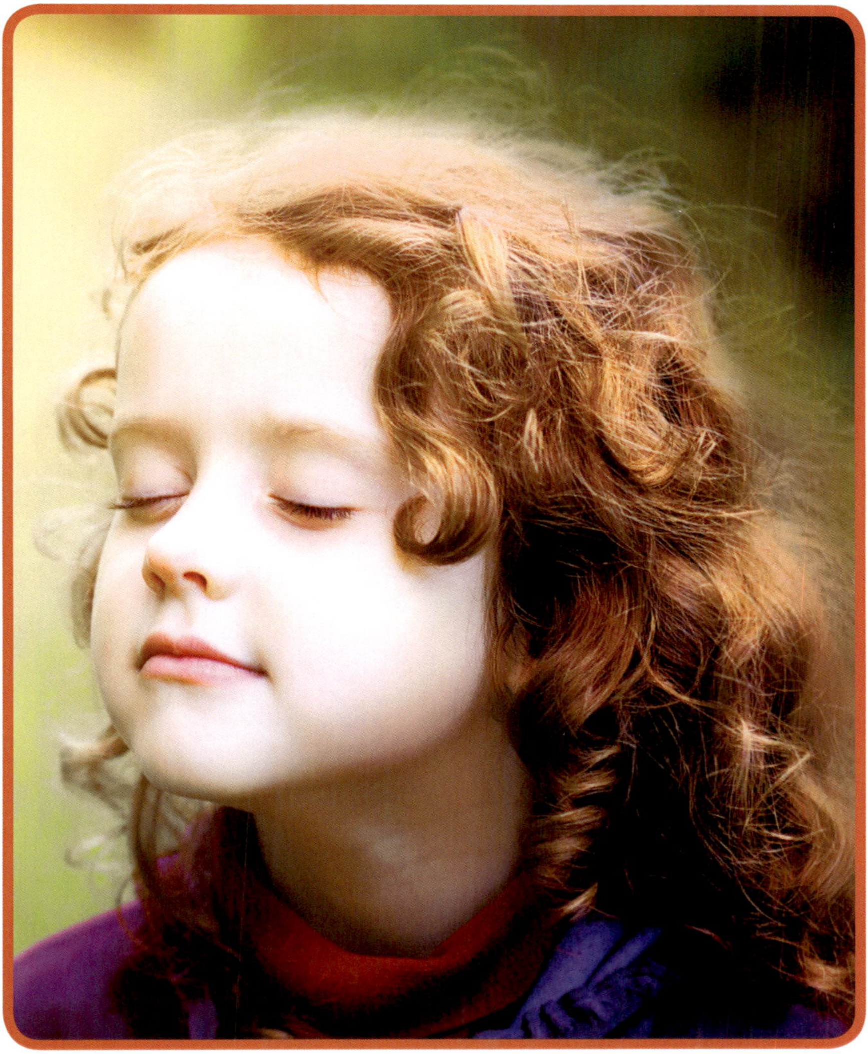

I can breathe.

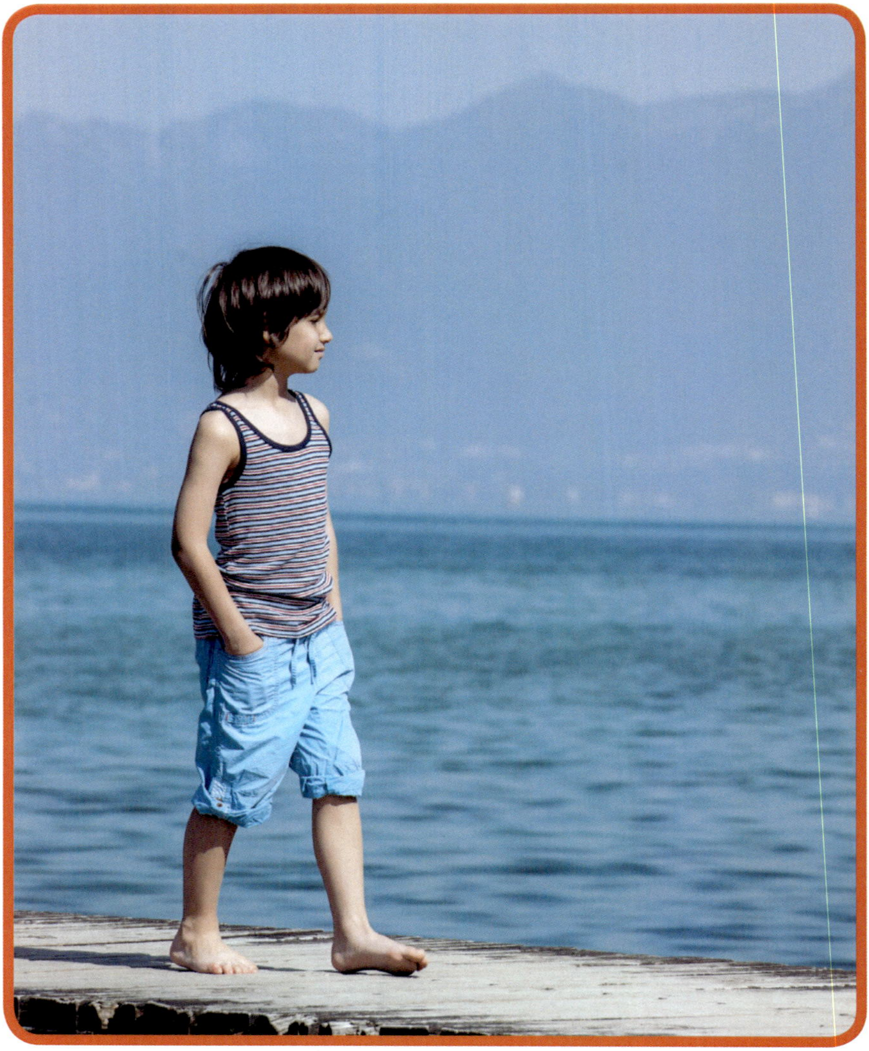

I can walk.

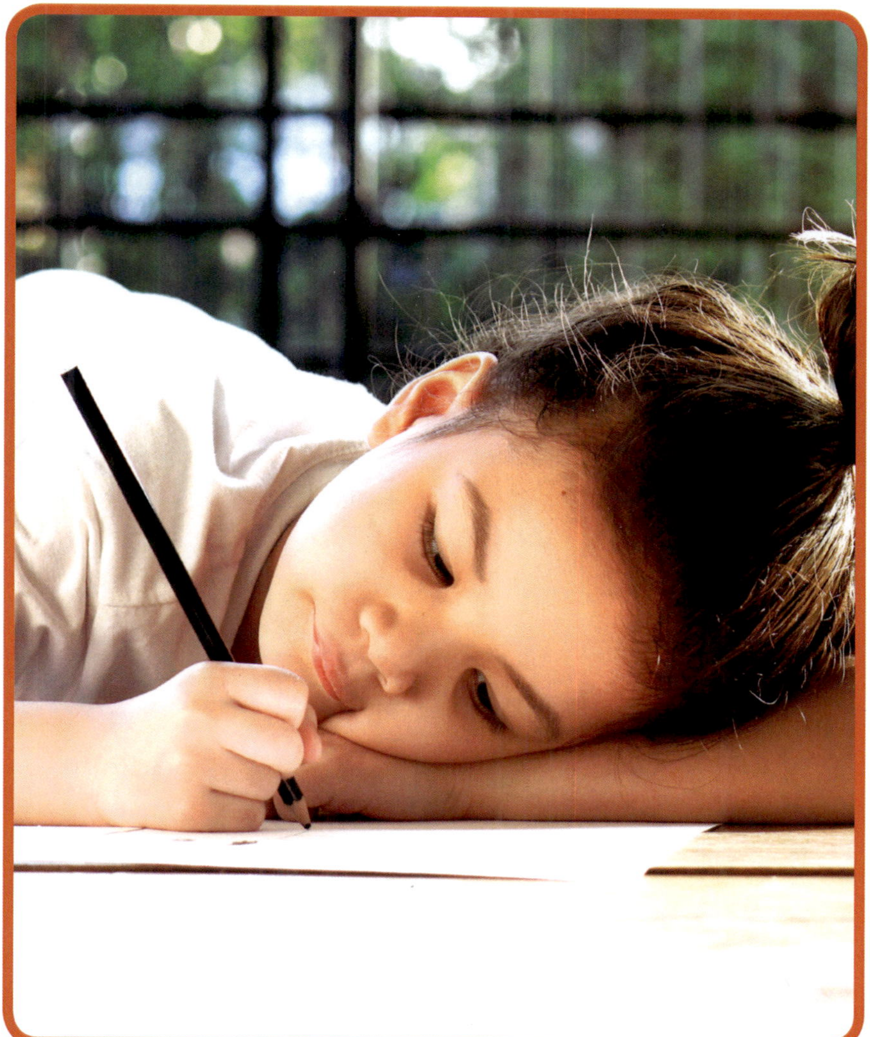

I can draw.

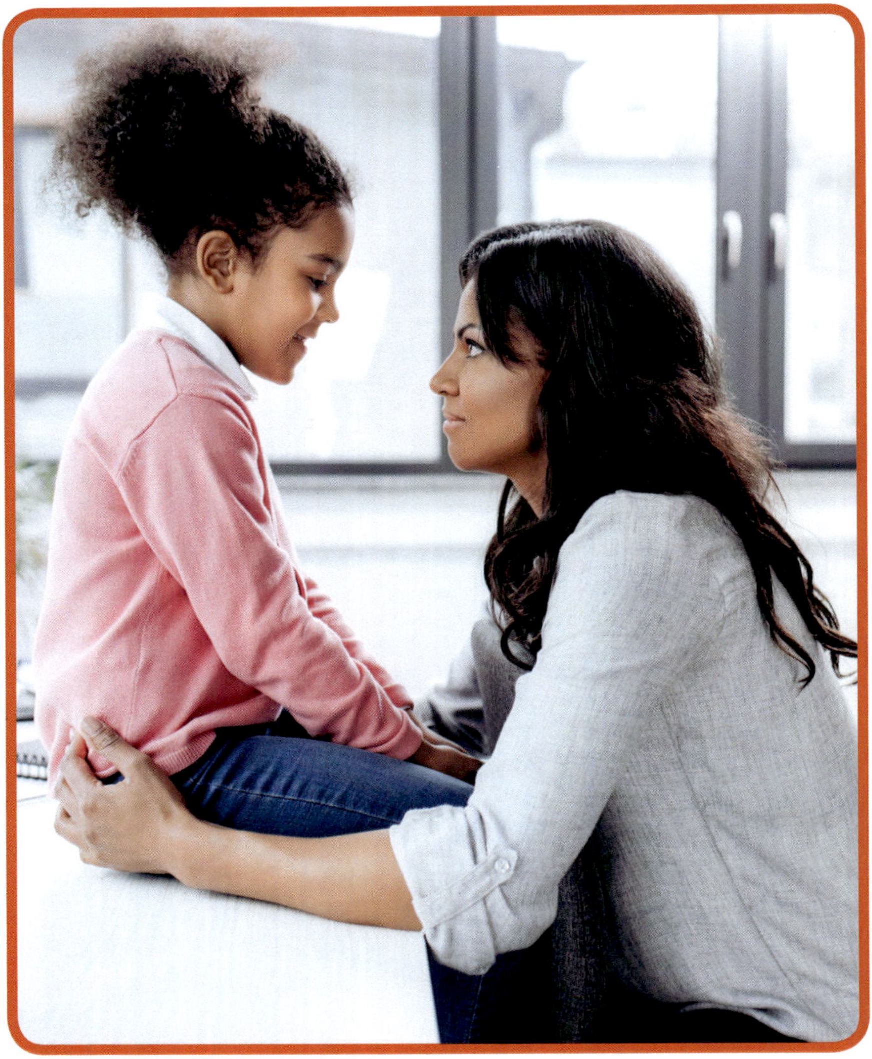

I can talk.

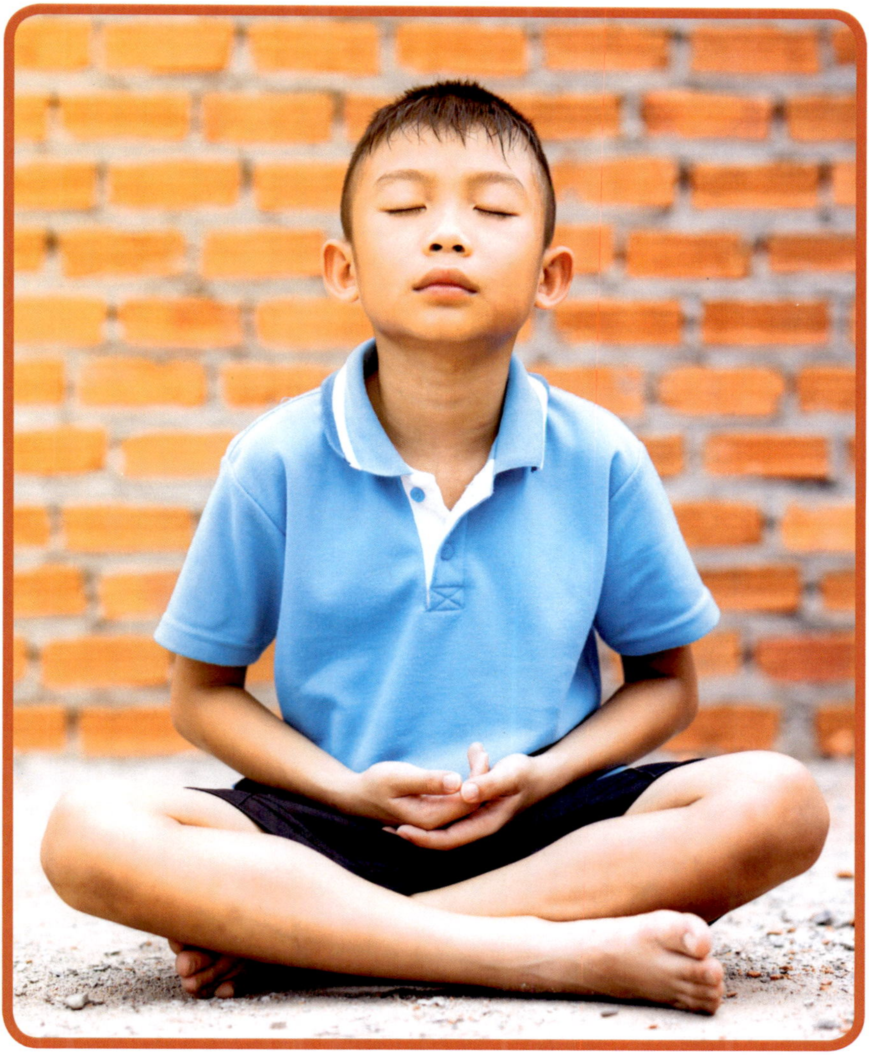

I am calm.

Words to Know

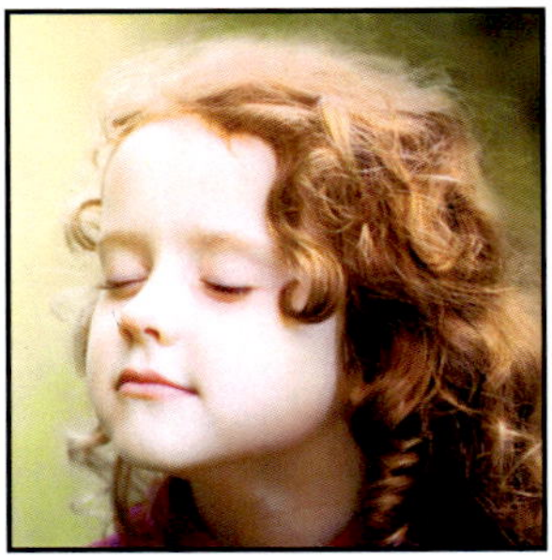

breathe

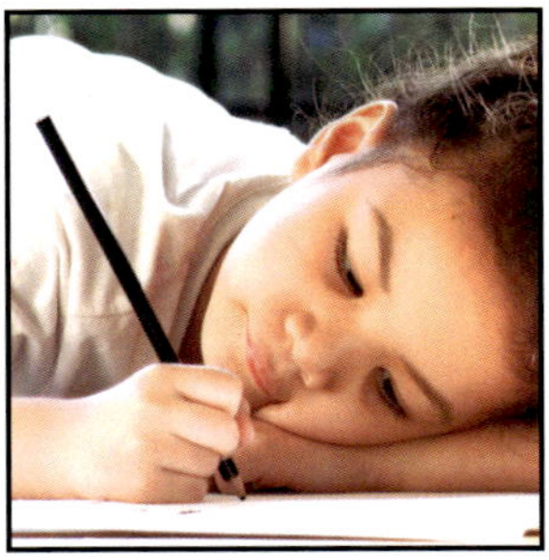

draw

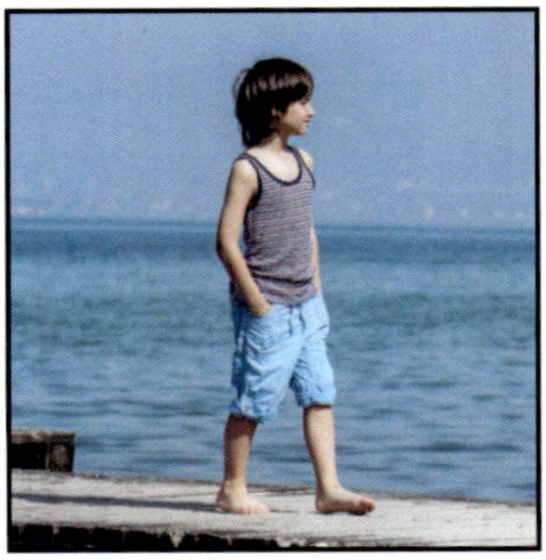

walk